Acoustic Guitar
The Big Book of Fun and Easy Tunes

Frederick Johnson
Copyright © 2019 Frederick Johnson

All rights reserved.

Frederick Johnson

Chords Used in this Book
[use as reference]

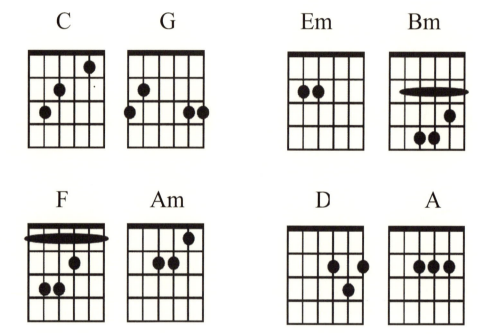

CONTENTS

1. Introduction (1)

2. Tablature (9)

3. Chords & Progressions (15)

4. Picking (21)

5. Fun and Easy Tunes (23)

Acoustic Guitar For Kids
The Big Book of Fun and Easy Tunes

INTRODUCTION

Welcome to this introductory course in acoustic guitar basics. Congratulations on selecting the most incredible of all stringed instruments - the acoustic guitar - which revolutionised pop and rock music and changed the world of music. You too can start a legacy as a musician and hopefully, this book will prove to be a useful tool and invaluable starting point.

This book has two goals: to get you started on the acoustic guitar from day one and to five you an extensive range of beginner songs to start out with. If you follow every lesson and instruction from each chapter, you'll have a head start in your guitar learning.

Before playing a single note though, we have to tune up. Tuning the guitar takes time and patience especially when starting out. With months and years of experience, you'll be able to tune without the help of a tuner. A point that must be emphasised right from the start is that tuning has to be absolutely precise. Don't settle for an approximation. In this way, once you've tuned each string, go back and ensure the strings are in tune a second time before playing.

Every song in this book uses what we call **standard tuning**. Standard tuning is the basic guitar tuning that most players use. It is the tuning which the guitar was built to hold and withstand. In heavier genres like the many varieties of metal and some forms of punk, alternate tunings are used. These include drop tunings like Drop D and Drop B. These are not relevant in a beginner's guide to the acoustic guitar, but it is useful to be aware of their existence nonetheless.

Standard Tuning is:

              E   A   D   G   B   E

We tune the guitar from the low string (E) to the high string (E). The lowest E is the one nearest to you. This is also the thickest string. There are some great youtube videos with tuners which let you match the note. Alternatively, you could purchase a guitar tuner which fits on the headstock of the guitar and ready to go. However, in this day and age, it's more practical to just find a free tuner online and tune up before playing.

Now that you are in tune, let's take a look at the components of the acoustic guitar. Getting to know your instrument is the most important step that you can take when beginning your guitar journey. This is for health and safety and also for the reason that when you understand the ins and outs of your instrument, you can proceed to having a better comprehension for how to get the best sound out of it.

On the page opposite, we have an annotated diagram of an acoustic guitar with labels so that you can see what's what. Acoustic guitars are one of the three main guitar types: electric, acoustic and classical. Of course, hybrids of the instruments exist but traditionally, these are the three varieties. Nowadays, most major guitar manufacturers have an electronic EQ system built into acoustic guitars with a pickup. These are electro-acoustic guitars and are extremely useful when in concert or recording through an interface.

Acoustic Guitar

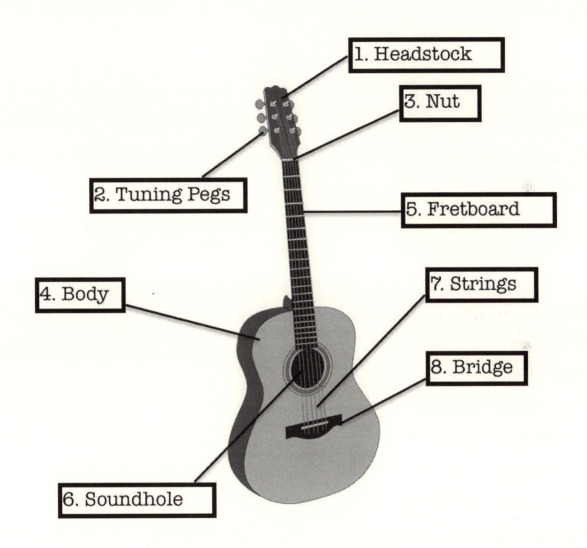

Index

1. Headstock

The function of the headstock is to contain the tuning pegs and is where we tune the guitar. It also is designed to balance the instrument's weight appropriately with the neck and body. The headstock is where you will typically find the name of the brand of your instrument.

The headstock is a fragile part of the guitar which you should avoid knocking or hitting at all costs. This point cannot be emphasised enough. Damage can vary from your guitar no longer staying in tune to a dented neck or even fret and nut problems. Any of these will cost you a lot of money, especially since luthiers are not cheap nowadays and if your guitar cost a lot, you'll be looking at further charges. It's best to take precautionary measures and look after your instrument. Purchase a gig bag or case for all transportation.

2. Tuning Pegs

There are six tuning pegs on the guitar, one for each string. Just like its electric counterpart, the tuning pegs are extremely sensitive and so when you are tuning your instrument, especially if you got your instrument new with no setup and loose strings, be extremely cautious as guitar strings snap HARD if you tune incorrectly and are careless. Tune each peg slowly, turning them progressively - never in quick motions.

3. Nut

The nut is often overlooked and some players do not take into consideration just how pivotal this little bit of material really is. The nut is the linking point between the strings, bridge and headstock. It contains six individual slits where the strings sit on. Damage to the nut is as bad as damage to the headstock, if not worse. What you must appreciate as a guitarist is that while the nut seems futile, those individually spaced slits have been measured apart in a precise way down to the last millimetre. It is actually one of the most strenuous and laborious aspects of the craftsmanship that goes into fabrication of the instrument. When replacing strings, take your time and if you are ever unsure, have them replaced by your local music shop. Better to be safe than sorry.

4. Body

The most prominent feature of your guitar: its wonderful body. Look after it and ensure to dust it from time to time. Dust culminates a lot on the body's outer rim, the headstock and underneath the strings. Just like with any part of the instrument, ensure no physical damage occurs on it and love your instrument like you love any other personal expensive property.

5. Fretboard

The fretboard is the actual part of the instrument that your notation is played on. If you are right-handed, your left hand navigates this part of the instrument. Ensure the frets (individually lined notes) are not sharp and are smooth. If there are any issues, make sure to address them professionally before playing as injuries are frequent in poorly constructed and set up guitars. Most guitar stores will be able to sort out minor issues. The fretboard sits on the neck which your hand grasps as you play.

6. Soundhole

The sound hole is pretty self explanatory. It's where sound emits out of the instrument when played. On acoustic guitars, it's where many people accidentally drop their picks into (***plectrum'*** for our lovely British and Australian readers). Nonetheless, be sure that nothing is inside the sound hole as this can impair performance and the overall sound of your instrument.

7. Strings

Let's now talk about the strings of the guitar. There are so many different types of acoustic guitar string. We recommend always going for mid-range strings that emphasise the warmth of the instrument. However, only you know what sounds best for your style of playing. Just be sure to ask a guitar store employee if you are not sure about what strings to use/are appropriate for your guitar. One particular variety which has become popular in recent years is the phosphor bronze coated kind. These strings are long lasting and have a beautiful ring to them which makes your guitar sound like twice its price point and can enhance your playing, even if you're starting out.

Be aware that your strings should never feel too tight against the fretboard of the guitar. There should be an ease where you are able to press down on each fret and bend the strings a little bit. A maintenance tip is to purchase a guitar cleaning kit. These are inexpensive and usually contain conditioner. Keeping your strings clean is essential for hygiene and a crisp sounding instrument. Alternatively, use a duster and dab a small amount of water on a tea towel to regularly clean your fretboard and strings.

Changing your strings:

1. Unscrew the pins from the bridge of the guitar. In order to do this, you'll need a universal guitar set-up appliance.

2. Remove the old strings but pushing them up from under the bridge. On the headstock end, untie and unwind the strings and with precaution, pull them out.

3. Wipe down your instrument with a cloth to get rid of dust and prepare for the new strings.

4. Insert the ball end of the new strings into the sockets of the bridge. Put the pins in right away and securely fasten by pushing down and ensuring the string won't pop out.

5. Insert the sharp end of the strings into their respective tuning pegs and tune with precaution.

8. Bridge

The bridge is what holds the strings in place on the opposite end of the guitar to the headstock. Don't mess around with this part of the instrument as much like the other components which involve maintaining correct string tension, it is extremely delicate. You might note that the strings come out of holes in the bridge. This is normal and when you learn to string the guitar yourself, you'll find out better how the mechanism works.

In essence, each string has a ball on the end. You unscrew are tied in a knot on the bridge and unlike guitars, there are no pinned 'slots' in the bridge where you can insert strings into easily. This means that changing strings is not something you should try at home unless you are proficient in ukulele string replacement. Ask a guitar or music shop to do this for you when you do eventually buy new strings.

READING TABS

The housekeeping is out of the way and you are ready to learn how to play guitar. In this section, we will be tackling chords but before getting into chord shapes and where to place your fingers, we need to address how guitarists read music.

```
E|--------------------------------|
B|--------------------------------|
G|--------------------------------|
D|--------------------------------|
A|--------------------------------|
E|--------------------------------|
```

This diagram above is a 'tab', short for tablature and it is what we use in guitar music to indicate where we should place our fingers and what note to play. The E at the top of the diagram is the high string of the guitar and the E at the bottom is the low E and so, tabs are read from the bottom up and not the top up. The number on the string indicates the fret we play on the fretboard. Therefore, a '0' indicates that we are to play an open string without pressing on the fretboard. The diagram above shows how we tune a guitar: by playing each string open to match the E A D G B E standard tuning.

Another example:

```
E|--------------------------------|
B|--------------------------------|
G|--------------------------------|
D|---------------3----------------|
A|---------------3----------------|
E|---------------1----------------|
```

In the above diagram, we see that the G, B and high E strings are not in use so we DO NOT play them. The chord above is called an F power chord which means it is a short version of the long F chord. This is our first chord.

Step 1: Place your index finger on the first fret of the low E string.

Step 2: Place your ring finger on the third fret of the A string.

Step 3: Place your pinky on the third fret of the D string.

Step 4: Strum (with your right hand) the top three strings being careful not to play the high three.

This is a power chord and the shape that your fingers are in can be transposed anywhere on the fretboard to create different power chords, which are essential for riffs, which we will come to later.

Moving the same shape up from the first fret to the third fret creates a G power chord. It looks like this:

```
E|------------------------------|
B|------------------------------|
G|------------------------------|
D|---------------5--------------|
A|---------------5--------------|
E|---------------3--------------|
```

The E power looks like this:

```
E|------------------------------|
B|------------------------------|
G|------------------------------|
D|---------------2--------------|
A|---------------2--------------|
E|---------------0--------------|
```

The A power chord looks like this:

The B power chord looks like this:

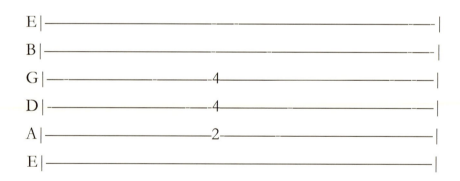

The D power chord looks like this:

```
E|-----------------------------------|
B|-----------------------------------|
G|-------------------7---------------|
D|-------------------7---------------|
A|-------------------5---------------|
E|-----------------------------------|
```

CHORDS & PROGRESSIONS

Let us slow things right down though. The reason I showed you power chords early on is because they are the easiest version of any chord you might need to use. But before taking another step, you need to learn the most basic chord progression which all beginner guitarist use: C, G, Am, F.

A chord progression is a series of (usually 3 or 4) chords which are played over and over in a song. Hundreds of thousands of pop and rock songs use the generic C, G, Am and F progression which is why it is essential to learn. Practice songs are included later on in the book so try to master this progression in this section before advancing to tackling anything more complex.

We are starting with a C major chord, or simply what we call 'C'. This going to be the basis for the entire exercise. It will take time and energy to master the progression itself so while I would usually say to focus on every chord individually, it is worth giving the entire progression a shot once you are somewhat comfortable with each chord.

The earlier on that you start practicing, the easier it will become.

C MAJOR CHORD

Here we have the C chord. It looks daunting but one needn't worry because everything is explained step by step.

Step 1: You want to get your fingers in the right position so you can start to memorise the chord shapes. You will start by placing your ring finger (fourth finger) on the third fret of the A string.

Step 2: Next, put your middle finger on the second fret of the D string. I understand that this feels like a close tuck and it is. Therefore, really push down so that the notes can ring out when you strum later.

Step 3: Leaving the G string open and untouched (hence the 0 in the diagram), place your index (pointer) finger on the first fret of the B string.

This is the C major shape. Truth be told, it will feel uncomfortable and maybe even painful when you first become acquainted with this chord shape. But the practice pays off because after a while you will be able to do a C major chord shape without thinking twice. It's all about practice and muscle memory.

This is the first chord of the four chord sequence. Now, we must advance to the G major chord.

G MAJOR CHORD

The G major chord is one of the reasons you should be learning guitar: in and of itself. It is wholesome, melodic and overall a gorgeous sounding chord.

Step 1: To start creating the shape, place your middle finger on the third fret of the low E string.

Step 2: Next, place your index finger on the second fret of the A string.

Step 3: Place your ring finger on the third fret of the B string and your pinky under it on the third fret of the high E string.

Once more, this position is not exactly the most fun for a beginner and it is a big jump from C to G. Nonetheless, it is a pivotal chord to learn for any genre of music. I urge you not to give up though, no matter how hard you find playing it. Perseverance is key.

A tip regarding this chord is that if you find the high notes difficult to keep down i.e. your ring and pinky on the B and E strings, then just try playing the top four strings and progressively introducing the high notes.

A MINOR CHORD

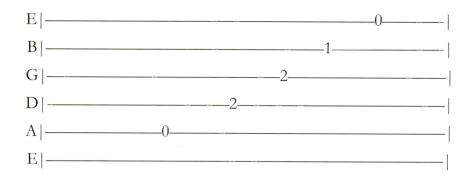

Every chord progression needs a good minor chord to bring it together. No chord does this more so than A minor. Unlike the other chords in this progression, this one does not use the low E string so when you play it, start out slow ensuring not to hit that low string.

Step 1: Place your middle finger on the second fret of the D string.

Step 2: Place your ring finger under it on the second fret of the G string.

Step 3: Finish the chord shape with your index finger on the first fret of the B string.

Step 4: Strum the chord using all strings except the low E.

F MAJOR CHORD

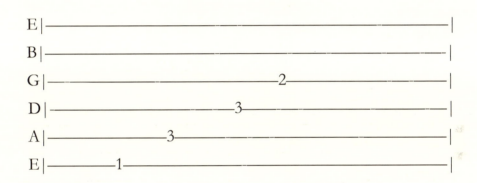

The F major chord is by far the hardest chord that a beginner could come across. The full shape using a technique called barring but since this book is designed as an introductory text for beginners, we will focus on the simplified version. Earlier, we came across the F major power chord. The F chord is very similar but more extensive.

Step 1: Place your index finger on the first fret of the E string.

Step 2: Place your ring finger on the third fret of the A string.

Step 3: Place your ring finger on the third fret of the D string.

Step 4: Finish by placing your middle finger on the second fret of the G string.

So now that you have the tools for your first chord progression, it's time for you to practice, practice, practice! Do not take another step until you have mastered each of the four chords and can comfortably change between them. Once you have nailed each chord, try playing them in this easy sequence:

    C   C   C   C   G   G   G   G

Am Am Am Am   F   F   F   F

The purpose of this exercise is to get you into a groove or rhythm of playing. It's one thing to learn to play the notes and another thing entirely to make it into music.

PICKING

What must be addressed is picking/strumming. Picking patterns are an essential part of playing the guitar and make riffs/chords sound either amazing or terrible. When starting out on guitar, most players pick downwards on every stroke. This works for some riffs but upstrokes are just as important. When writing out picking patterns, guitarists use D (down pick) and U (up pick) to signify what sort of picking is used. Try picking in alternate picking patterns like these:

D   D   U   D   D   U

In this picking pattern, you will pick the strings in a 'down, down, up' pattern i.e. two down picks and one up pick. This is a great beginner's pattern as it only involves one up pick.

D   U   D   D   U

Similar to the previous pattern, this one is slightly more challenging but you can master it with a bit of practice.

These are the primary two picking patterns used for playing chords and riffs. When you practice more and you get the hang of riffing, the picking pattern of a song will come naturally to you. The whole idea of a picking pattern is to make the riff run smoothly without breaks which can make a guitarist sound amateur and unprofessional. It's similar to a violinist who learns how to bow properly and fluidly.

Guitarists must learn as early as possible how to pick appropriately. On the occasion, you might find that some songs and riffs have multiple possibilities for picking patterns and there isn't only one right way of playing the song. This is fine too and in these cases, it is just a matter of what feels best for you.

Some songs start on an up-pick. While rare, I would encourage you to practice any of the riffs in this book with an up-picked start. What happens when you try this is your muscle memory improves because you are taking on a technique which isn't natural. What *is* natural when you start playing a riff is to down pick from the start. Alternating shouldn't be a huge aspect of your practicing but it should be included nonetheless. You'll thank your future guitarist self for giving this a go earlier on in your musical career.

FUN AND EASY TUNES

Joy to the World

Chords Used :

G C D

[Verse]

G   D   G
Joy to the world, the Lord is come!

  C   D   G
Let earth receive her King;

   G   G   G
Let every heart prepare Him room,

  G   G
And Heaven and nature sing,

  D   D
And Heaven and nature sing,

    G   C   G D G

And Heaven, and Heaven, and nature sing.

[Verse]

  G   D   G

Joy to the earth, the Saviour reigns!

    C   D   G

Let men their songs employ;

   G   G   G

While fields and floods, rocks, hills and plains

   G   G

Repeat the sounding joy,

   D   D

Repeat the sounding joy,

   G C   G D G

Repeat, repeat, the sounding joy.

[Verse]

G		D	G

He rules the world with truth and grace,

   C   D   G

And makes the nations prove

   G   G   G

The glories of His righteousness,

   G   G

And wonders of His love,

 D   D

And wonders of His love,

   G   C   G D G

And wonders, wonders, of His love.

[Verse]

```
G           D   G
```
Joy to the world, the Lord is come!

```
 C   D      G
```
Let earth receive her King;

```
  G     G     G
```
Let every heart prepare Him room,

```
  G         G
```
And Heaven and nature sing,

```
 D         D
```
And Heaven and nature sing,

```
 G      C     G D G
```
And Heaven, and Heaven, and nature sing.

[Verse]

```
G           D   G
```
He rules the world with truth and grace,

   C   D   G
And makes the nations prove

   G   G   G
The glories of His righteousness,

   G   G
And wonders of His love,

   D   D
And wonders of His love,

   G   C   G D G
And wonders, wonders, of His love.

Itsy Bitsy Spider

Chords Used :

G D C

G

Itsy bitsy spider

D   G

Went up the water spout.

G

Down came the rain and

C   G

Washed the spider out.

[Verse]

G

Out came the sun and

D   G

Dried up all the rain

And the itsy-bitsy spider

D G

Went up the spout again.

[Verse]

G

The itsy-bitsy spider

D G

Spun a spiral web

G

Caught a grasshopper

C G

Whose life began to ebb

[Verse]

G

Sucked up the juices

D   G

And grew a size that day

So the itsy-bitsy spider

D   G

Rebuilt the web array

[Verse]

G

The itsy bitsy spider

D   G

Laid a clutch of eggs

G

Out hatched the spiderlings

C   G

Each with all 8 legs

[Verse]

G

Spun a little web

D   G

And ballooned into the sky

So the itsy bitsy spider

D   G

Was happy then to die

Hot Cross Buns

Chords Used :

G C D

G D G

Hot cross buns!

G D G

Hot cross buns!

G   D

One a penny, two a penny,

G D G

Hot cross buns!

[Verse]

G   D

If you have no daughters,

D   G

give them to your sons.

G   D

One a penny, two a penny,

G   D   G

Hot cross buns!

[Chorus]

G   D   G

Hot cross buns!

G   D   G

Hot cross buns!

G   D

One a penny, two a penny,

G   D   G

Hot cross buns!

[Verse]

G   D

Butter them and sugar them and

D   G

put them in your mouth

  G   D

One a penny, two a penny,

  G D G

Hot cross buns!

[Chorus]

  G D G

Hot cross buns!

  G D G

Hot cross buns!

  G   D

One a penny, two a penny,

  G D G

Hot cross buns!

This Land Is Your Land

Chords Used :

G A D

      G   D

This land is your land, and this land is

my land

      A   D D

From California, to the New York

Island

      G   D

From the Redwood Forest, to the Gulf

stream waters,

A   D

this land was made for you and me

    G   D

As I was walking a ribbon of highway

    A   D D

I saw above me an endless skyway

    G   D

I saw below me a golden valley

A   D

This land was made for you and me

    G   D

This land is your land, and this land is

my land

    A   D D

From California, to the New York

Island

    G   D

From the Redwood Forest, to the Gulf

stream waters,

| A | D |

this land was made for you and me

| G | D |

I've roamed and rambled and I've

followed my footsteps

| A | D | D |

To the sparkling sands of her diamond

deserts

| G | D |

And all around me a voice was

sounding

| A | D |

This land was made for you and me

| G | D |

This land is your land, and this land is

my land

    A   D D

From California, to the New York

Island

      G   D

From the Redwood Forest, to the Gulf

stream waters,

A   D

this land was made for you and me

     G   D

The sun comes shining as I was

strolling

      A   D D

The wheat fields waving and the dust

clouds rolling

     G   D

The fog was lifting a voice come

chanting

 A   D

This land was made for you and me

      G   D

This land is your land, and this land is

my land

    A   D D

From California, to the New York

Island

       G   D

From the Redwood Forest, to the Gulf

stream waters,

|A| |D|
this land was made for you and me

|G| |D|
As I was walkin' - I saw a sign there

|A D D|
And that sign said - no tress passin'

|G| |D|
But on the other side .... it didn't say nothin!

|A| |D|
Now that side was made for you and

me!

|G| |D|
This land is your land, and this land is

my land

|A D D|
From California, to the New York

Island

      G   D

From the Redwood Forest, to the Gulf

stream waters,

A   D

this land was made for you and me

        G   D

In the squares of the city - In the

shadow of the steeple

      A   D D

Near the relief office - I see my people

    G   D

And some are grumblin' and some are wonderin'

  A   D

If this land's still made for you and me.

```
     G             D
This land is your land, and this land is

my land

     A          D   D
From California, to the New York

Island

        G            D
From the Redwood Forest, to the Gulf

stream waters,

A                D
this land was made for you and me

A                D
this land was made for you and me.
```

My Country Tis' Of Thee

Chords Used :

D   A   D

_____

D   A   D   A

D
My country 'tis of thee, sweet land of

liberty, of thee I sing.

D   A
Land where my fathers died, land of the

pilgrim's pride.

D   A   D
From every mountain side let freedom

ring!

D   A   D   A

D
My native country, thee, land of the

noble free, Thy name I love.

D   A
I love thy rocks and rills, Thy woods

and templed hills.

D   A   D
My heart with rapture thrills like that

above.

D   A   D   A

D
Let music swell the breeze, and ring

from all the trees sweet freedom's song.

D   A
Let mortal tongues awake, let all that

breathe partake.

D   A   D

Let rocks their silence break, the sound

prolong.

D   A   D   A

D

Our father's God, to Thee, Author of

liberty, to Thee we sing.

D   A

Long may our land be bright with

freedom's holy light.

D   A   D

Protect us by Thy might, Great God, our King!

D   A   D   A

D
My country 'tis of thee, sweet land of

liberty, of thee I sing.

D   A
Land where my fathers died, land of the

pilgrim's pride.

D   A D
From every mountain side let freedom

ring!

D A D   A

D
My native country, thee, land of the

noble free, Thy name I love.

D   A
I love thy rocks and rills, Thy woods

and templed hills.

```
   D              A      D
My heart with rapture thrills like that

above.


   D     A       D           A


D
Let music swell the breeze, and ring

from all the trees sweet freedom's song.

   D          A
Let mortal tongues awake, let all that

breathe partake.

   D           A    D
Let rocks their silence break, the sound

prolong.


   D     A    D       A
```

D

Our father's God, to Thee, Author of

liberty, to Thee we sing.

D			A

Long may our land be bright with

freedom's holy light.

D			A	D

Protect us by Thy might, Great God, our

King!

Ba Ba Black Sheep

Chords Used :

G D C

[Verse]

G   D

Baa baa black sheep

C   G

Have you any wool

C   G

Yes sir yes sir

D   G

Three bags full

[Verse]

G   C

One for the master

G D
One for the dame

  G C
And one for the little boy

  G D G
Who lives down the lane

[Verse]

G   C
Thank you says the master

G   D
Thank you say the dame

  G C
And thank you says the little boy

  G D G
Who lives down the lane.

I Can Sing a Rainbow

Chords Used :

G   C   Am   D   Bm

[Verse]

G   Bm

Red and yellow and pink and green

C   G   Am   D

Orange and purple and blue

G   C   G   C

I can sing a rainbow sing a rainbow

G   D   G

Sing a rainbow too

[Bridge]

C   G

Listen with your eyes

C   G

Listen with your eyes

  C C G

And sing everything you see

A   D A D

You can sing a rainbow sing a rainbow

A   D D

Sing along with me

[Verse]

G   Bm

Red and yellow and pink and green

C G Am D

Orange and purple and blue

G C G C

I can sing a rainbow sing a rainbow

G D G

Sing a rainbow too

B-I-N-G-O

Chords Used :

C   F   G   Am

     C   F   C

There was a farmer had a dog,

    C   G   C

And Bingo was his name-o.

C   F

B-I-N-G-O

G   C

B-I-N-G-O

Am   F

B-I-N-G-O

    G   C

And Bingo was his name-o.

    C   F   C

There was a farmer had a dog,

    C   G   C

And Bingo was his name-o.

C   F

B-I-N-G-O

G   C

B-I-N-G-O

Am   F

B-I-N-G-O

   G   C

And Bingo was his name-o.

Humpty Dumpty

Chords Used :

C F G

C   F   C

Humpty Dumpty sat on the wall,

C   F   C

Humpty Dumpty had a great fall.

C

All the king's horses

C

And all the king's men

F

Couldn't put Humpty Dumpty

F   C

Together again.

C	F	C

Humpty Dumpty sat on the wall,

C	F	C

Humpty Dumpty had a great fall.

C

All the king's horses

C

And all the king's men

F

Couldn't put Humpty Dumpty

C

Together again.

Jack and Jill

Chords Used :

C   F   G

 C   G

Jack and Jill went up the hill

 C   G

To fetch a pail of water

C   G

Jack fell down and broke his crown

 C G C

And Jill came tumbling after

C   G

Up Jack got and home did trot

 C   G

As fast as he could caper

    C   G
And went to bed and bound his head

     C   G   C
With vinegar and brown paper

C   G
Then Jill came in and she did grin

   C   G
To see Jack's paper plaster

   C   G
Her mother whipped her 'cross her knee

   C   G   C
For laughing at Jack's disaster.

Hokey Pokey

Chords Used :

C   F   G

      C

You put your right foot in

You put your right foot out

You put your right foot in

    G

And you shake it all about

You do the hokey pokey and you turn yourself around

        C

That's what it's all about!

     C

You put your left foot in

You put your left foot out

You put your left foot in

      G

And you shake it all about

You do the hokey pokey and you turn yourself around

          C

That's what it's all about!

Mary Had a Little Lamb

Chords Used :

G   D

G   D   G

Mary had a little lamb, little lamb, little lamb

G   D   G

Mary had a little lamb, it's fleece was white as snow

G   D   G

Mary had a small camel, small camel, small camel

G   D   G

Mary had a small camel, it's hump was very round

G   D   G

Mary had a little lamb, little lamb, little lamb

G   D   G

Mary had a little lamb, it's fleece was white as snow

G   D   G

Mary had a small camel, small camel, small camel

```
G              D           G
```
Mary had a small camel, it's hump was very round

```
G              D        G
```
Mary had a little lamb, little lamb, little lamb

```
G              D           G
```
Mary had a little lamb, it's fleece was white as snow

```
G              D        G
```
Mary had a small camel, small camel, small camel

```
G              D           G
```
Mary had a small camel, its hump was very round.

Row Your Boat

Chords Used :

G Em C D

[Verse]

G   Em   C   G

Row, row, row your boat

G   Em   D

Gently down the stream

G   D   G   C

Merrily, merrily, merrily, merrily

D   G   G

Life is but a dream

[Verse]

G   Em   C   G

Row, row, row your boat

G   Em   D

Gently up the creek,

G   D   G   C

If you see a little mouse

D   G   G

Don't forget to squeak!

[Verse]

G   Em C   G

Row, row, row your boat

G   Em   D

Gently down the stream,

G   D   G   C

If you see a crocodile

D   G   G

Don't forget to scream!

[Verse]

| G | Em | C | G |

Row, row, row your boat

| G | Em | D |

Gently to the shore

| G | D | G | C |

If you see a Tiger there

| D | G | G |

Don't forget to roar!

Three Blind Mice

Chords Used :

C G

  C   G   C

Three blind mice

C   G   C

Three blind mice

C G   C

See how they run

C G   C

See how they run

C   G   C

They all ran after the farmer's wife

        G   C

Who cut off their tails with a carving knife

       G   C

Have you ever seen such a sight in your life

  C   G   C
As three blind mice.

 C   G   C
Three blind mice

 C   G   C
Three blind mice

C G   C
See how they run

C G   C
See how they run

 C   G   C
They all ran after the farmer's wife

          G   C
Who cut off their tails with a carving knife

        G   C
Have you ever seen such a sight in your life

  C   G C
As three blind mice.

Twinkle Twinkle Little Star

Chords Used :

G   D

[Verse]

    G

The wheels on the bus go round and round,

D   G

Round and round, round and round

The wheels on the bus go round and round,

D   G

All through the town

[Verse]

    G

The money on the bus goes clink, clink, clink,

D   G

clink, clink, clink,   clink, clink, clink.

The money on the bus goes clink, clink, clink,

D   G

All through the town.

[Verse]

    G

The wipers on the bus go swish swish swish

D   G

Round and round, round and round

The wheels on the bus go round and round,

D   G

All through the town

[Verse]

    G

The driver on the bus goes "Move on back!"

D   G

Round and round, round and round

The wheels on the bus go round and round,

  D   G

All through the town

[Verse]

     G

The people on the bus go up and down

D   G

Round and round, round and round

The wheels on the bus go round and round,

D   G

All through the town

[Verse]

     G

The horn on the bus goes beep beep beep

D   G

Round and round, round and round

The wheels on the bus go round and round,

   D   G

All through the town

[Verse]

     G

The baby on the bus goes "Wah wah wah!"

   D   G

Round and round, round and round

The wheels on the bus go round and round,

   D   G

All through the town

[Verse]

     G

The parents on the bus go "Sh sh sh"

   D   G

Round and round, round and round

The wheels on the bus go round and round,

 D   G

All through the town

[Verse]

      G

The wheels on the bus go round and round

 D   G

Round and round, round and round

The wheels on the bus go round and round,

 D   G

All through the town.

I'm a Little Teapot

Chords Used :

G C D

G

I'm a little teapot

C   G

Short and stout

C   G

Here is my handle

D   G

Here is my spout

G

When I get all steamed up

C   G

I just shout

C   G   D   G

"Tip me over and pour me out"

G

I'm a little teapot

C   G

Short and stout

C   G

Here is my handle

D   G

Here is my spout

G

When I get all steamed up

C   G

I just shout

C   G   D   G

"Tip me over and pour me out".

Head, Shoulders, Knees & Toes

Chords Used :

C   F   G

[Verse]

C

Head and shoulders knees and toes, knees and toes

C   G

Head and shoulders knees and toes, knees and toes

    C   F

And eyes and ears and mouth and nose

G   C

Head and shoulders knees and toes

[Verse]

C

Feet and tummies arms and chins, arms and chins

C	G

Feet and tummies arms and chins, arms and chins

C	F

And eyes and ears and mouth and shins

G	C

Feet and tummies arms and chins

[Verse]

C

Hands and fingers legs and lips, legs and lips

C	G

Hands and fingers legs and lips, legs and lips

C	F

And eyes and ears and mouth and hips

G	C

Hands and fingers legs and lips

[Verse]

C

Head and shoulders knees and toes, knees and toes

C   G

Head and shoulders knees and toes, knees and toes

    C   F

And eyes and ears and mouth and nose

G   C

Head and shoulders knees and toes.

Old MacDonald

Chords Used :

A   **E**   **D**

[Verse]

  A   D   A

Old MacDonald had a farm,

A   E   A

Ee i ee i oh!

  A   D   A

And on that farm he had some chickens,

A   E   A

Ee i ee i oh!

     D   D   A

With a cluck-cluck here,

     D   D   A

And a cluck-cluck there

A	D

Here a cluck, there a cluck,

A	D	D

Everywhere a cluck-cluck

A	D	A

Old MacDonald had a farm

A	E	A	A

Ee i ee i oh!

[Verse]

A	D	A

Old MacDonald had a farm,

A	E	A

Ee i ee i oh!

A	D	A

And on that farm he had some cows

A	E	A

Ee i ee i oh!

    D D A

With a Moo-Moo here,

 D D A

And a Moo-Moo there

A   D

Here a Moo, there a Moo,

A   D D

Everywhere a Moo-Moo

A   D   A

Old MacDonald had a farm

A E A A

Ee i ee i oh!

[Verse]

A   D   A

Old MacDonald had a farm,

A E A

Ee i ee i oh!

A D A

And on that farm he had a dog,

A E A

Ee i ee i oh!

  D D A

With a Woof-Woof here,

 D D A

And a Woof-Woof there

A D

Here a Woof, there a Woof,

A D D

Everywhere a Woof-Woof

A D A

Old MacDonald had a farm

A E A A

Ee i ee i oh!

[Verse]

   A   D   A
Old MacDonald had a farm,

A   E   A
Ee i ee i oh!

   A   D   A
And on that farm he had some ducks,

A   E   A
Ee i ee i oh!

      D   D   A
With a Quack-Quack here,

      D   D   A
And a Quack-Quack there

  A   D
Here a Quack, there a Quack,

  A   D   D
Everywhere a Quack-Quack

   A   D   A

Old MacDonald had a farm

A E A A

Ee i ee i oh!

[Verse]

   A   D   A

Old MacDonald had a farm,

A E A

Ee i ee i oh!

   A   D   A

And on that farm he had some Sheep,

A E A

Ee i ee i oh!

     D D A

With a Baa-Baa here,

     D D A

And a Baa-Baa there

   A   D

Here a Baa, there a Baa,

   A   D D

Everywhere a Baa-Baa

   A   D   A

Old MacDonald had a farm

A E A A

Ee i ee i oh!

   A   D   A

Old MacDonald had a farm,

A E A

Ee i ee i oh!

  A   D   A

And on that farm he had some Pigs,

A E A

Ee i ee i oh!

    D D A

With an Oink-Oink here,

    D D A

And an Oink-Oink there

A   D

Here an Oink, there an Oink,

A   D D

Everywhere an Oink-Oink

A   D A

Old MacDonald had a farm

A   E E A   A E   A

Eeeeee i , eeeeee i , — oh.

The Alphabet Song

Chords Used :

A E D

   A   A
A   B   C   D   E   F   G

   D   D   A
H   I   J   K   L   M   N   O   P

   D   E   D   E
Q   R   S   T   U   V   W   X   Y and Z

   A   D   E   A
Now I know my ABCs, next time won't you sing with me !

Here is the tablature version of the song for those who are more daring and ambitious:

```
E|-----------------------------------------------|
B|-----------------------------------------------|
G|-----------------------------------------------|
D|-----------------------------------------------|
A|—0—0—7—7—9—9—7-------------------------------|
E|-----------------------------------------------|


E|-----------------------------------------------|
B|-----------------------------------------------|
G|-----------------------------------------------|
D|-----------------------------------------------|
A|—5—5—4—4—2—2—2—2—0---------------------------|
E|-----------------------------------------------|


E|-----------------------------------------------|
B|-----------------------------------------------|
G|-----------------------------------------------|
D|-----------------------------------------------|
A|—7—7—5—4—4—2—7—7—5—4—4—2---------------------|
E|-----------------------------------------------|
```

```
E|---------------------------------------------|
B|---------------------------------------------|
G|---------------------------------------------|
D|---------------------------------------------|
A|--0--0--7--7--9--9--7-----------------------|
E|---------------------------------------------|


E|---------------------------------------------|
B|---------------------------------------------|
G|---------------------------------------------|
D|---------------------------------------------|
A|--5--5--4--4--2--2--0--2--------------------|
E|---------------------------------------------|
```

Manufactured by Amazon.ca
Bolton, ON